SOULFUL ADVENTURES

SOULFUL ADVENTURES

Nurturing Your Mind in the Modern World

HAIRDRESSING MUM

Soulful Adventures:
Nurturing Your Mind in the Modern World
Hairdressing Mum

First Edition, 2023

Table of Contents

Introduction

Greetings, fellow seekers of soulful enlightenment! Get ready to set off on an adventure into the depths of your own mind, as together we fly through the pages of this captivating mindfulness guide.

Welcome to *Soulful Adventures: Nurturing Your Mind in the Modern World*, where we need to change into our super-suits to discover the powers of a balanced, resilient, and joy-filled life. Buckle up because this is not your ordinary self-help guide. This is a grand adventure that will ignite your spirit and soothe your soul!

In a world buzzing with distractions and bustling with chaos, we'll uncover the hidden gems of mental well-being. Our journey will teach us about meditation, yoga, mindfulness, and self-care, unravelling their secrets and embracing their transformative power. But fear not! This is not a journey for the serious and stoic. We're here to infuse our expedition with a sense of empowerment and boundless enthusiasm!

Soulful Adventures will be your trusty compass, guiding you through the labyrinth of modern life with whimsy and wisdom. We'll unravel the intricate tapestry of science behind these practices, all the while painting vivid landscapes of imagination and inspiration. This is a book where learning meets joy, and where growth and exploration go hand in hand.

Picture yourself soaring through the pages as we uncover the magic of self-compassion, the art of quietening the mind, and the sheer bliss of savouring life's simplest pleasures. From the gentle warmth of a sunrise to the exhilaration of dancing in the rain, we'll celebrate the extraordinary in the ordinary and rediscover the wonder that lies within each passing moment.

Soulful Adventures invites you to unleash your inner hero, to rise above the noise and tap into the spring of your own resilience and potential. We'll equip you with practical tools and playful exercises that will light your path, guiding you towards a life brimming with purpose, fulfilment, and self-discovery. Forget needing a hero, become the superhero of your own life!

So, my fellow adventurers, get ready to embark on a journey like no other. Grab your metaphorical superhero cape and prepare to glide through the landscapes of your own soul. Together, we'll explore the intricacies of modern life, nurturing our minds and reclaiming our sense of wonder. Are you ready to dive into *Soulful Adventures: Nurturing Your Mind in the Modern World*? Let the quest begin!

Throughout this book we will pause and be present with new thoughts to explore and tasks to add to your daily life, so have a pen and paper at the ready. Before you start, write down the hours of your day, let's say from 7am to 11pm, then as you read this book and come across a new suggested activity, write it on your paper at the easiest time. By the time you finish the book, you will have a new-found 'me-time' sheet at your disposal ready for you to start discovering a clear mind and nurtured soul.

Chapter 1

Unveiling the Modern Mind: Conquering Inner Peace

In this first chapter, we tackle the challenges of the modern world that mess with our peace of mind. From being glued to our screens to feeling overwhelmed by too much information, it's a wild ride. We'll discover why taking care of our mental health is essential and explore cool ways to find balance and harmony.

It's time to test your stamina and strength as we are going to conquer the challenges that come with living in today's fast-paced world. Our minds are bombarded with constant distractions and demands, leaving us feeling stressed and overwhelmed. But have no fear, for we hold the power to unlock our inner peace.

Picture this: you're constantly surrounded by screens, notifications, and never-ending to-do lists. It seems like there's never a moment to breathe, let alone find time for yourself. I'm sure it isn't a struggle to imagine this feeling as it is the everyday life you are living right now! The modern mind is a bustling hub of information, constantly processing, multitasking, and struggling to keep up. As you read this, your first step is to stop for just a minute and realise that you are not alone in feeling like this. This never-ending treadmill is a byproduct of the new world we are all living in. Yes, there is self-help advice available, but there is so much that it's overwhelming knowing where to start, when in fact all it takes is a little self-love and self-worth, setting small boundaries as you listen to your soul.

Amidst the chaos, it's time that we discover a powerful truth: taking care of our mental health is crucial. It's not a luxury or an afterthought – it's a necessity. We must prioritise our well-being to thrive in this dynamic world.

Now, let's uncover some secrets to conquer those challenges that repeatedly assail our peace of mind. It's time to equip ourselves with tools to navigate this rollercoaster ride called life.

Together, we'll delve into the art of finding balance in the modern era. We'll explore how the fast-paced nature of our lives affects our mental well-being and understand the importance of tending to our minds and souls. We'll discuss the impact of constant connectivity and information overload, which can leave us feeling drained and disconnected. We'll acknowledge the pressures we face, both external and internal, and the toll they take on our mental health.

But don't worry, for we're not here to dwell on the challenges alone. We're here to be empowered through the use of practical tools and insights to navigate this complex landscape.

On this adventure, we'll discover how the art of quietening the mind can be our guiding light. This offers us refuge, peace, and a deep connection with ourselves.

So, let's unlock the secrets to conquering our inner peace amidst the madness of the modern world. We'll cultivate resilience, embrace self-care, and build meaningful connections along the way.

Are you ready to undertake this mission to achieve your transformation? Grab your super-suit, for the adventure awaits. Let's unveil the potential of the modern mind and discover the boundless possibilities that lie within.

Navigating Constant Connectivity

In the realm of constant connectivity, finding moments of tranquillity can feel like searching for a needle in a haystack. However, here are some ways to navigate this digital labyrinth and reclaim your peace of mind.

Establish Digital Boundaries:

First, we need to set clear boundaries for your digital engagement. Designate specific times to check emails and social media and resist the temptation to be constantly available – go on, add this to your new daily 'me time' sheet. Remember, your mental well-being takes priority over virtual distractions.

Research shows that around 70% of people open their eyes in the morning and reach straight for their phones. This instantly fills our minds with the external world through emails, news updates, and social media, and doesn't give us a minute to process our own natural conscious thoughts. To allow our brains to connect with the present and to start making small adjustments in the way we think, closing our eyes and stopping thoughts when they arise helps us to focus on the present moment and understand self-awareness. This can be a very positive change in our daily routine, boosting creativity and problem solving, enhancing memory and reducing stress levels. The result is to stop letting the digital world interrupt and control our daily thoughts.

Prioritise Rest and Sleep:

Make quality sleep a priority by establishing a consistent bedtime routine and creating a peaceful sleep environment. Remember, a well-rested mind is better equipped to face life's challenges. Instead of scrolling through social media posts or YouTube reels before you sleep, try finding a positive mindset podcast or video that you can listen to as you drift off, soothing your mind and clearing it of outside clutter.

Start tomorrow morning. Change your routine just slightly so that when the early morning alarm goes off, you will leave your phone right where it is. Get out of bed and head to a window or even out into your garden if you have one. Give yourself 5 minutes of inner peace and quiet and enjoy the gentle warmth of the sunrise. The morning daylight is a super way to recharge your batteries full of positivity. Don't worry, you can go to the kettle first to make your first brew of the day before you step out into the sunlight. Just remember, do not take your phone, tablet or laptop with you! This should be your first of your daily inputs on your 'me-time' planner. So, if you start your day at the usual time of 7am, write down a 6.30am entry to set an alarm and, when it goes off, get straight out of bed. Head to the morning sun and find that moment of peace.

The same can be said for the television – if your daily routine consists of flicking on the TV to listen to the morning news and other external information, pause. Instead, keep the house and your mind quiet for just those first 5 minutes. Then over the next few days, expand those 5 minutes to 10, then 20, even if this means setting that morning alarm before the rest of your household wakes up. Complete the first week with this little change as part of your routine and you will quickly feel pride in yourself and be ready to accept these changes for the future you.

Practise Digital Detoxes:

Throughout your day, take regular breaks from screens to rejuvenate your mind. Engage in activities that nourish your soul, such as going for a walk, reading a book, or spending quality time with loved ones. Disconnecting from the digital world can help you reconnect with yourself. Pause for a minute, check your timesheet and pick just one hour in your day where you forbid yourself from reaching for digital distractions. As you grow into a more mindful version of you, this hour can easily multiply.

When you complete a task at work, household jobs, or even when catching up with a friend or watching TV, do you find that your mind wanders, your phone vibrates, and before you know it, you have lost full concentration on the job at hand or enjoying a moment of socialising, and you're now scrolling through Facebook or watching pointless videos?!

This is not a productive or positive way to live and over time, our brains become altered and attention spans shorten. Simple alterations to your phone's notification settings can quickly change this. Turn off all unimportant app notifications so you only see these irrelevant messages when you choose to open an app. Do this now! Just don't get distracted: complete this task and come straight back.

Well done, you are learning and changing your ways already.

Try a new habit of putting your phone on silent before you start a task, then go a step further and put it down in a designated place out of sight until your task is complete. These simple and small habit changes to tackle modern technology will soon help you feel more present, and believe me, you will discover much more enjoyment in everything you do.

Confronting Information Overload

In the era of information overload, it's easy to feel overwhelmed and scattered. However, with mindful practices and intentional choices, you can regain control and clarity.

1. **Filter Your Inputs:** Selectively curate the information you consume. Choose reliable sources and limit exposure to excessive news or social media that may trigger anxiety or negativity. Focus on what's essential and relevant to you.

Tips

Go through your social media accounts and delete contacts that are constantly sharing negative statuses and information. Seeing this all the time seeps into your mind and tricks your brain into believing that only negative things happen in the world. There is so much positivity in life, you just have to look in the right places!

Search through the accounts you follow and take a minute to reflect on what they bring to your life. If an account is filled with negative unwanted information or you find yourself judging or comparing yourself, get rid of it! You can always follow them again should you want to.

Search for some happy thoughts. In your social media search bars, type keywords like, 'law of attraction', 'happy minds', 'fun', 'positive vibes', 'strong mindset' and follow some of the profiles you like the look of. Then, if a part of your daily habits involves scrolling through feeds and watching reels, you will soon find yourself easily and effortlessly soaking up more positivity throughout your day.

2. **Practise Mindful Consumption:** Engage in mindful consumption by taking breaks from information overload. Cultivate the habit of mindful reading, listening, and watching. Ask yourself if the information you're absorbing is serving your well-being and contributing positively to your life.

Tips

Set time limits on certain apps you use on a daily basis. This works as a reminder that you are spending time on something you are mindfully aware that you don't want to be doing as much.

Set goals and times on a new or forgotten hobby, something such as reading, colouring, or even baking. Think back to times when you felt your happiest or calmest, so dust off that book you always said you wanted to read. Start with once a week or every other day and plan a small activity just for you. Remove distractions and enjoy the peace.

Plan a weekly or monthly games night with your family or friends. It's amazing how joyful you will feel sitting around the table among your loved ones with a little fun competition involved. Keep the phones and gadgets away from the table and embrace the present moment as you play.

This first chapter has taken us on a journey through the bustling hub of the modern mind, a place where constant distractions and overwhelming demands have become the norm. But in the midst of this chaos, we've uncovered a profound truth: Taking care of our mental well-being is not just a luxury but an absolute necessity. It's the key to thriving in a fast-paced world that never seems to slow down.

We've explored the challenges posed by constant connectivity and information overload, recognising the toll they can take on our inner peace and mental clarity. However, this chapter is not merely about dwelling on these challenges; it's about empowerment. It's about providing you with practical tools and insights to navigate your overloaded wandering mind. We've also touched on the significance of confronting information overload, taking time away from our electronic devices, curating the information we consume and engaging in mindful practices that contribute positively to our well-being.

So, as we move forward into the heart of this expedition, let's remember that our adventure has only just begun. We're here to summon our inner superhero, the brave, determined, and driven version of us, to cultivate resilience, embrace self-care, and build meaningful connections with ourselves and others. The potential of the modern mind is boundless, and the possibilities that lie within are waiting to be unveiled. Put on your superhero cape and together we'll conquer the challenges of the modern world and find the inner peace and balance we so deeply deserve.

Chapter 2

The Power of Modern Meditation: Calming the Chaos

Get ready to tap into the incredible power of modern meditation! We'll uncover simple techniques that fit into our fast-paced lives. Meditation isn't just about sitting still and saying "Om." It's a superpower that can zap away stress and help us to focus and understand ourselves better. Get excited for a calmer, happier you!

Supercharge Your Mind with Modern Meditation

Welcome to the enchanting world of modern meditation! In this chapter, we'll explore the fascinating realm of meditation and its profound impact on our brains and overall well-being. Through the lens of neuroplasticity, we'll unveil the remarkable ability of our brains to adapt and reorganise in response to our experiences.

The Science Behind Meditation: A Beginner's Guide

Meditation has long been practised and revered for its ability to bring peace and clarity to the mind. But what does science have to say about this ancient practice? Let's explore the easy-to-understand science behind meditation and uncover the fascinating benefits it offers.

Neuroplasticity and Brain Reshaping:

- Regular meditation practice can quite literally reshape our brains. Through the phenomenon of neuroplasticity, meditation enhances grey matter density in areas associated with attention, emotional regulation, and self-awareness. This transformative power allows us to become more focused, emotionally resilient, and self-aware.

Stress Reduction through Cortisol Control:

- Meditation's well-documented ability to reduce stress is evident. By lowering cortisol levels, meditation serves as a natural antidote to the stress and anxiety prevalent in modern life. It calms the mind and triggers the body's relaxation response, offering a sanctuary of peace.

Enhancing Cognitive Abilities:

- In a world filled with distractions, meditation becomes a valuable tool for enhancing cognitive abilities. Regular practice can improve attention span, working memory, and cognitive flexibility. By training our minds to stay present and focused, meditation equips us to navigate information overload and excel in various cognitive tasks.

Emotional Well-being and Happiness:

- Research has shown that meditation profoundly increases positive emotions while decreasing negative ones, leading to an overall improvement in mood and happiness.

Mindfulness practices foster a greater awareness of our thoughts and emotions, empowering us to respond to them with skill and compassion.

Boosting Immune Function:

- Surprisingly, meditation also positively affects our physical health. The mind-body connection really has the power to regulate our well-being and meditation harnesses its benefits. By reducing inflammation, enhancing cellular health, and fortifying the immune system, meditation supports our overall health.

As you can see, the science behind meditation is compelling. From reshaping the brain to reducing stress, enhancing cognitive abilities, fostering emotional well-being, and boosting immune function, meditation offers a wealth of benefits for both the mind and body. So, why not give it a try? Start with just a few minutes a day, and gradually build up your practice. With time and consistency, you may find yourself experiencing the transformative power of meditation firsthand.

<u>The Meditation Marvels</u>:

Imagine meditation as a superpower that can zap away stress and bring peace to your mind. It's not just about sitting cross-legged and touching your thumbs and forefingers together. It's a simple yet powerful practice that can transform your life.

<u>Mini-Meditations for Busy Beginners:</u>

Don't worry, you don't need hours of spare time to meditate. We'll explore bite-sized meditation techniques that fit perfectly into your fast-paced life. From one-minute breathing exercises to mindful moments during daily activities, you'll discover that even a few moments of stillness can make a world of difference. It's like a secret potion for your brain!

Are you ready to discover your inner superhero powers through the amazing world of meditation? Well, grab your cape, take a deep breath, and like a true superhero, let's go!

Step 1: Find Your Secret Hideout
Every superhero needs a secret hideout, right? So, find your Batcave where you can meditate without villainous distractions. Lighting some candles, playing relaxing music, and turning out the lights are good ways to make it your fortress of solitude!

Step 2: Get Comfortable Like a Superhero in HQ
Strike a pose that would make even the mightiest superhero proud! Whether you sit like a cross-legged Zen Master, rule from your meditation throne (a comfy chair) or lie down like you're floating on clouds, find a position that lets you relax while staying alert.

Step 3: Activate Your Intention
Every superhero has a mission, and now it's your turn. Set an intention for your meditation adventure. It could be to unleash inner peace, banish stress, or simply stay present in the moment. Your intention will be your guiding star on this heroic journey!

Step 4: Breath Control
Time to harness your breath. Feel each breath flow in and out of your body. Imagine your breath is your superpower, grounding

you in the present like a mighty anchor. Inhale strength and serenity, exhale stress and distractions!

Step 5: Mindful Mode

As thoughts sneak in, acknowledge them without judgment, and then send them packing! Return your focus to your breath or pick a point of focus – a meditation mantra, an image in your mind, or the tingling sensation of your body awakening. Embrace the moment with determination!

Step 6: Start with Short Steps

Even superheroes start with small victories! Begin your meditation with short sessions, around 5 or 10 minutes, and then gradually level up your meditation powers. Remember, it's not about the duration; it's about consistently practising your new-found powers every day!

Step 7: Guided Meditations

Need some help with your meditation? Explore guided meditations! They're like your trusty sidekicks, guiding you through your meditation quests. These pre-recorded audio or video sessions provide step-by-step instructions and gentle reminders to guide your practice. Numerous apps and online resources offer a variety of guided meditations to suit you.

Step 8: Power Up with Gratitude

Before you conclude your meditation, power up with gratitude like a true superhero. Reflect on three things in your life that make your heart swell with appreciation, then repeat to yourself 'Thank you, thank you, thank you'. Gratitude is your secret power boost!

Step 9: Carry Your Zen Everywhere
Don't leave your superpowers behind! Take your meditation mojo with you everywhere you go. Use mindfulness in your daily adventures. Savor every moment, embrace every challenge, and let your positive presence shine like a beacon of light!

With this fun guide, you're all set to activate your superpower of self-discovery. As you follow these steps, you'll unlock your inner superhero and become a force of positivity, peace, and all-around awesomeness. So, go for it, believe in yourself and open your mind to change. May your meditation adventure be as epic as your superhero dreams!

The Mindful Walk: A Journey of Inner Discovery
Let's try "The Mindful Walk" meditation experience, where we embark on a serene stroll that leads us to the heart of mindfulness. Find yourself a peaceful outdoor space, one where it feels like the world slows down just for you.

Step 1: Grounding and Breathing
Start by standing still, like a mighty tree planting its roots. Inhale deeply, feeling the energy of the Earth beneath you. Exhale slowly, releasing any tension. Take another deep breath, envisioning yourself ready for this mindful quest.

Step 2: The First Step of Awareness
As you take your first step, immerse yourself in the sensation of your feet feeling the Earth. Feel the gentle touch of the ground beneath you, welcoming your presence. Let your feet become sensors of the Earth's texture and energy.

Step 3: The Dance of Movement
Continue your leisurely walk, embracing the natural rhythm of your body. Watch how your legs move gracefully with each step, and how your arms sway rhythmically, in perfect harmony with your stride.

Step 4: Harmonise Your Breath
Now, sync your steps with your breath. Inhale deeply, feeling the fresh air filling your lungs. As you exhale, imagine releasing any stress or worries. Let the rise and fall of your chest become a strength, filling you with calmness and tranquillity.

Step 5: Awaken Your Senses to the World
As you journey onward, open your senses to the world around you. See the vibrant tapestry of nature's beauty, the powerful colours and shapes that paint the world before you. Listen to the melodies of nature's orchestra, the whispering leaves, the singing birds, and the gentle rustling of life.

Step 6: Return to the Present Moment
Should your thoughts wander, gently guide them back to the moment and the rhythm of your breath. Embrace this opportunity to be fully present.

Make this adventure last. Set aside at least 20 minutes of your day to enjoy this mindful mission and don't let the weather stop you, you can perform your mindful walk and turn it into a dance in the rain.

Step 7: A Grateful Conclusion
As we reach the end of this mindful journey, pause for a moment and express gratitude. Give thanks for the simple act

of walking, for the profound connection it nurtures between you and the world. Slowly, let your walk come to a gentle stop, taking one final deep breath, and as you exhale, feel at one with the universe.

Through this, you've tapped into your inner superhero, embracing the art of being fully present in each heroic step and breath. Carry this new-found heroism with you as you continue your day, knowing that you can always return to this place of inner strength and serenity.

You can practise "The Mindful Walk" whenever you desire to reconnect with the present moment. May your walks be a source of meditation, joy, and rejuvenation.

Remember, meditation is a personal journey, and each experience is unique. Be patient and kind to yourself as you explore this practice. You may find that the first few times you practise meditation you will tell yourself you can't do it, your mind is too busy, you can't concentrate, but in fact, you can! Anyone can meditate and you, my reader, can do anything you want to do, you just have to don your superhero cape and believe in yourself. Embrace the simplicity and joy of modern meditation, knowing that it holds the power to transform your mind and bring you closer to inner peace. Meditation is not something many of us are introduced to early in life or are educated about, so it may feel unusual to implement it, but you would be surprised how many people use it on a daily basis and for how many thousands of years it has been practised.

Your Journey to Inner Peace

Congratulations, brave soul, for pursuing this journey to discover the power of modern meditation! You now hold the power to unlock a world of calmness and serenity amidst the chaos. Savour the simplicity and joy of meditation, making it a part of your daily routine.

Remember, meditation is not about being perfect or achieving some elusive state of mind. It's about showing up for yourself, even if it's just a few moments each day. Take pleasure in the fun and ease of modern meditation, and watch as it transforms your life from the inside out. Your inner superhero is ready to bask in the peaceful bliss of your mind's sanctuary.

Chapter 3

Finding Balance and Connection Through Yoga: The Awesome Body-Soul Dance

Imagine a mind and body dance party! That's yoga, my friend. We'll explore how yoga is another way for you to feel like a superhero. Stretching, moving, and breathing come together in beautiful harmony to make you feel strong and centred. It's not just about bending into different positions; it's about connecting with yourself and the world around you. Get ready to strike a pose and feel amazing!

Simplified yoga science

Imagine your body as a superhero and yoga is its trusty sidekick. Together, they form an unbeatable team that brings balance and peace to your entire being. Through the science of yoga, we'll explore how it unleashes a series of incredible superpowers within you.

First, let's dive into the brain. Yoga has been scientifically proven to be a secret weapon at rewiring your brain, helping you become more focused and calmer. It's like a mental power-up that enhances your memory, concentration, and problem-solving skills. Say goodbye to brain fog and hello to mental clarity!

But that's not all – let's move on to your body. Flexibility is one of yoga's greatest secrets. As you stretch and twist into different poses, your muscles and joints become more flexible, just like a superhero's incredible elasticity. Not only does this make you feel amazing, but it also helps prevent injuries and keeps your body agile and youthful.

But wait, there's more! Yoga taps into the power of your body's energy centres known as chakras. These spinning wheels of energy hold the key to unlocking your inner potential. By balancing and aligning your chakras through yoga, you'll feel an extraordinary surge of vitality and harmony coursing through your entire being.

Science has also discovered that yoga boosts your immune system, helping you fight off villains like colds and infections. It's like injecting your immune system with a mega-boost, making you feel invincible.

Let's give it a go!

The Joy of Mindful Yoga Practice 1: Sun Salutations (Surya Namaskar)

Step 1: Mountain Pose (Tadasana)
Stand tall with your feet together, arms at your sides, and palms facing forward. Take a deep breath and centre yourself.

Step 2: Upward Salute (Urdhva Hastasana)
Inhale, lift your arms overhead, and bring your palms together. Gently arch your back and look up, feeling the stretch in your spine.

Step 3: Forward Fold (Uttanasana)
Exhale, bend at the hips, and fold forward. Bend your knees if needed and let your head and hands hang towards the ground.

Step 4: Halfway Lift (Ardha Uttanasana)
Inhale, lift your torso halfway, lengthening your spine. Place your hands on your shins or fingertips on the ground, keeping your gaze straight ahead.

Step 5: Plank (Phalakasana)
Exhale, step or jump back to a high plank position. Align your wrists under your shoulders, engage your core, and keep your body in a straight line.

Step 6: Low Plank (Chaturanga Dandasana)
Lower your body down with control, bending your elbows and keeping them close to your ribs. Hold this position for a moment, engaging your core and your upper body strength.

Step 7: Upward-Facing Dog (Urdhva Mukha Svanasana)
Inhale, roll over your toes, and lift your chest and thighs off the ground. Press your palms into the mat, keeping your shoulders away from your ears.

Step 8: Downward-Facing Dog (Adho Mukha Svanasana)
Exhale, tuck your toes under, lift your hips, and form an inverted "V" shape with your body. Relax your head and neck, pressing your heels towards the ground.

Step 9: Repeat Steps 2-8 in reverse order to complete one full round of Sun Salutations.

The Joy of Mindful Yoga Practice 2: Tree Pose (Vrikshasana)

Step 1: Mountain Pose (Tadasana)
Stand tall with your feet hip-width apart and arms at your sides. Find your balance and ground yourself.

Step 2: Shift Your Weight to Your Left Leg
Shift your weight onto your left foot, keeping your toes grounded and your hips aligned. Step 3: Lift Right Foot and Place Sole on Inner Left Thigh or Calf Bring the sole of your right foot to rest on the inner left thigh or calf. Avoid placing it directly on the knee joint.

Step 4: Hands to Heart's Centre (Anjali Mudra)
Bring your hands together in a prayer position at your heart's centre. Find a steady focus point to help your balance.

Step 5: Find Stability and Lengthen Your Spine
Engage your core muscles to maintain stability. Lengthen your spine, gently lifting the crown of your head towards the ceiling.

Step 6: Explore Arm Variations

If you feel balanced, experiment with different arm variations. Extend your arms overhead, reach out sideways, or keep them at your sides for added stability.

Step 7: Breathe and Relax

Take deep breaths, allowing yourself to find calm and balance in the pose. If you waver or fall out of the pose, simply stop, reset and return to it.

Step 8: Repeat on the Other Leg

Note: Feel free to use a wall or a chair for support as you explore this pose. As you become more comfortable, challenge yourself by practising without support.

Now, close your eyes and take a deep breath. Feel that? Yoga has a magical effect on your breath. It teaches you to take slow, deep breaths that send signals to your brain, telling it to relax. It's like casting a spell that banishes stress, anxiety, and worries, leaving you feeling calm and at peace.

Enjoy Your Yoga Journey

Remember, these are just a couple of simple yoga practices to get you started. Explore different poses, flows, and sequences that resonate with you. Embrace the joy of movement, find delight in the present moment, and listen to your body's needs. As you incorporate yoga into your life, you'll discover its ability to bring about physical well-being, mental clarity, and a deeper connection with yourself. Enjoy your yoga journey and let it be a source of joy, rejuvenation, and inner peace.

Author's Note:
As the writer of this chapter, I want to emphasise that while I am not a trained professional in yoga, my intention is to share accessible and enjoyable yoga practices with you. These practices are based on my personal experiences and research. It's important to approach yoga with an open mind, listen to your body's limitations, and seek guidance from a certified yoga instructor if needed. Remember, yoga is a personal journey, and what matters most is finding joy, self-expression, and mindful movement that suits your unique needs. Enjoy the exploration and let your yoga practice be a source of pleasure and prosperity in your life.

Chapter 4

Quietening the Mind: Embracing Inner Peace

In this chapter, we'll discover the art of quietening our busy minds. It's like hitting the mute button in the middle of a crazy movie. We'll explore fun techniques like journaling, immersing ourselves in nature and utilising the skills we learnt in Chapter 1 to take breaks from our screens. Find your calm in the storm and embrace the peace within you.

Imagine your mind as a bustling city, filled with the noise of honking car horns, the flashing lights of billboards, and the never-ending chatter of passersby. Now, picture a superhero who possesses the power to bring calm and serenity. That superhero is you, armed with the science of quietening the mind and embracing inner peace. When you quieten your mind, it's like turning down the volume on all those noisy distractions. Scientifically speaking, it reduces the levels of stress hormones in your body, boosts your immune system, and improves your overall well-being. It's like hitting the reset button for your mind and body's stress. Discovering inner peace is like finding a secret oasis amidst the hustle and bustle. It allows you to recharge, find clarity, and discover your true self. Studies show that when you find inner peace, it positively impacts your relationships, creativity, and even your ability to handle challenges. So, put on your superhero cape, take a deep breath, and let the science of quietening the mind and embracing inner peace guide you to a state of blissful tranquillity.

Cultivating Mindfulness

Mindfulness is a powerful tool in our arsenal for conquering the challenges the modern mind has to tackle. By practising mindfulness, we can anchor ourselves in the present moment and cultivate a sense of peace and clarity.

1. **Mindful Breathing:** Take a few moments each day to focus on your breath. Observe the sensation of each inhalation and exhalation, allowing yourself to be fully present in its rhythm. It may feel a little strange at first if you haven't done this before, but very quickly it will become second nature as this simple practice can help calm the mind, promote a sense of centredness, and it can be used anywhere, at any time of day.

2. **Engage Your Senses:** Each day, tune into your senses and savour the simple pleasures of life. Whether it's the aroma of freshly brewed coffee, the feel of cool grass beneath your feet, or the sound of birds chirping, fully immerse yourself in the present moment and let your senses guide you into a state of mindfulness. Again, this can start as once a day (pick a time on your 'me-time' sheet) for you to stop yourself at any point in your hectic life and embrace the moment. A

good way to start these practices may be in your new morning routine as we explored in Chapter 1.

Fun Techniques to Calm the Mind: Embrace Serenity Through Playful Mindfulness Games

Who said quietening the mind had to be serious and solemn? Let's explore some fun techniques and playful mindfulness games that can help you find tranquillity with a smile on your face! Let's discover the joy of quietening the mind!

1. **The Sound of Silence:** Find a quiet spot and close your eyes. Listen attentively to the sounds around you – the chirping of birds, the rustling of leaves, or the distant hum of traffic. Challenge yourself to identify as many sounds as possible, fully immersing yourself in the symphony of the present moment. It's like a playful game of auditory exploration! Give it a go, you will soon find yourself smiling.

2. **Sensory Delight:** Engage your senses in a delightful sensory experience. Choose a small piece of chocolate, a fragrant flower, or a smooth pebble. Explore the texture, smell, taste, or colour of the object with childlike curiosity. Let the sensations captivate your attention and anchor you in the present moment. It's a sensory adventure that brings mindfulness to life and childhood memories may even arise. Sensory exploration can be a trip down memory lane as many of us remember happy memories from our youths – making perfume out of flower petals is still a favourite pastime of mine.

Dance with Breath

Who said meditation had to be still and motionless? Let's infuse some movement into our pursuit of inner peace.

1. **Flowing Breath:** Stand with your feet hip-width apart, and gently sway your body from side to side, allowing your breath to guide your movement. Inhale as you shift to one side and exhale as you shift to the other. Let your breath and body flow in harmony, releasing tension and inviting in tranquillity. It's a dance of breath and movement that calms the mind.

2. **Mindful Walking:** Take a mindful walk through nature or even around your own home. With each step, bring your full attention to the sensation of your feet touching the ground. Notice the feeling of the Earth, the gentle sway of your body, and the rhythm of your breath. Let your walk become a moving meditation, an opportunity to connect with the world around you. Return to Chapter 2 for a detailed explanation.

Creative Expression

Artistic expression can be a wonderful way to quieten the mind and tap into your inner creativity. Give these techniques a try:

1. **Meditative Doodles:** Grab a pen and a piece of paper. Allow your hand to move freely, creating shapes, patterns, and doodles without any specific goal in mind. Let your subconscious guide your hand, observing the lines and curves as they unfold. This playful and intuitive process can quieten the mind and spark your imagination. Just 5 minutes

of letting the pen find its way around your piece of paper can create inner peace.

2. **Mindful Colouring:** Appreciate the joy of colouring books designed for adults. Choose intricate patterns or mandalas and let the repetitive motion of colouring become a form of meditation. Focus on the sensation of the colours filling the page, letting go of any thoughts or worries. Allow the colours to bring you calmness and create a visual masterpiece.

Laughter Meditation

Laughter is truly the best medicine, and it can also be a powerful tool for quietening the mind.

1. **Laughter Yoga:** Gather your friends or simply find a space where you can relax. Start by fake laughing, and soon, the laughter becomes contagious and genuine. Allow yourself to laugh without inhibition, feeling the joy and lightness that laughter brings. This playful practice can release stress, uplift your spirits, and quieten the mind.

2. **Comedy Break:** Watch or listen to a comedy show, stand-up routine, or funny videos. Let yourself fully engage in the humour, allowing laughter to bubble up from within. Enjoy the moment of lightness as your mind relaxes and finds respite from your everyday concerns. Watching old children's movies can be super amusing too, as you will notice all the hidden adult humour you missed as a child!

3. **Journaling:** Journaling is a fun activity that can take on many creative styles. Here are some enjoyable journaling styles to try:

Art Journaling: Express your thoughts and feelings through visual art. Use drawings, paintings and collages to create pages of emotions and experiences.

Travel Journaling: Document your adventures. Include maps, photos, and sketches of the places you visit, along with your thoughts and reflections along the journey.

Gratitude Journaling: Cultivate a positive mindset by focusing on the things you're grateful for each day. Write down three things you appreciate, no matter how small or insignificant.

Letter Journaling: Write letters to your past or future self, or even people in your life. Pour your heart out or share your aspirations and address them as if you're sending or receiving a letter.

Treat yourself to a new notebook and even a shiny new pen. Journaling is your personal adventure. Find a cosy spot. Take a deep breath, reflect, and let your thoughts flow without judgment. Experiment with different styles. Be consistent. Use prompts for inspiration. Reflect on your entries. Journaling is self-care and self-discovery. Embrace the journey.

To conquer the challenges of the modern mind, learning to perform self-care becomes a vital part of our journey. It is through self-care practices that we nourish our souls and replenish our energy; it is the act of exploring physical activities that can bring us joy and promote our mental well-being. Whether it's practising yoga, going for a run, or dancing to your favourite tunes, find ways to move your body mindfully and connect with the present moment.

Quietening the mind doesn't have to be a serious and sombre affair. By infusing playfulness, movement, and creativity into our mindfulness practices, we discover that inner calm can be joyful and light-hearted. So, embark on this playful path, engage in mindful games, dance with your breath, express yourself creatively, and allow laughter to be your guide. In the realm of quietening the mind, fun and serenity go hand in hand.

By implementing these strategies, you can navigate the challenges of constant connectivity, information overload, and the demands of modern life. Remember, conquering the modern mind is a continuous practice. Take on the journey with curiosity, self-compassion, and a commitment to your well-being. After each short practice, make sure to praise yourself for the slight changes you've made, nothing is better for the soul than a little self-praise and self-recognition. Well done for giving change a try, we must break boundaries to see positive and heroic changes in our lives.

Chapter 5

Mindfulness in Everyday Life: Embracing the Present Moment

It's time to bring some mindful magic into your everyday life! We'll uncover the joy of being fully present in each moment. From savouring delicious food to moving with grace, we'll explore how mindfulness can make everything feel more vibrant and alive. Get ready to appreciate the little things and discover a whole new level of joy!

Imagine you have a time machine, and you can journey to any moment in the past or future. Pretty cool, right? Well, here's the catch: the most mind-blowing discoveries happen when you embrace the present moment. When you fully immerse yourself in the here and now, amazing things happen in your brain.

Scientifically speaking, embracing the present moment activates the prefrontal cortex, the part of your brain responsible for focus, creativity, and problem-solving. It's like a superhero power-up for your brain! Plus, being present allows you to savour life's little joys, like the taste of a delicious meal or the warmth of a hug. It's like capturing those magical moments in a time capsule. By embracing the present moment, you become a master of time and a conductor of happiness. So, ditch the time machine and soak up the present moment. Science says it's the place to be for a truly extraordinary and fulfilling life.

Embracing the Joy of the Present: Find Magic in Everyday Moments

Practise mindful activities: With everyday life being busy, leaving us feeling like we have a million and one tasks to do, sometimes we lose ourselves. At the end of the day, or at the end of a long journey, do you ever wonder, "How did I get here?" or "What have I done today?" or "Why do I feel so tired?" This is because you are not present in your mind, but rather rushing each task to get to the next. This isn't producing the best version of you. Tasks are completed with no enjoyment or effort, and you find everyone around you is looking happy and you're there with a hectic mind full of all the things you must do.

Let's change this. Engage in everyday activities with mindfulness. Whether it's washing dishes, walking your dog, or preparing a meal, infuse these moments with your complete attention.

Start this today. Each time you are washing your hands or washing the dishes, take a moment to feel the warmth of the water and feel gratitude for the luxury of clean running water flowing throughout your home. In everyday busy life, we forget how lucky we are to have what seem like small things, like fresh running water. In fact, if that was taken from you tomorrow and it became inaccessible, this small thing would immediately grow in importance. Giving thanks and thoughts of gratitude will soon have you realising how blessed you are.

Listen to the crunch of leaves beneath your feet. When out walking your dog or taking the children to school, take in the beauty of nature around you and realise how lucky we are to be alive on this beautiful planet. Slow your pace and just look around, take in the fresh air and beautiful surroundings of our world.

At dinner time, whether you are cooking for yourself or the whole family, take a moment to give thanks for the food we have available to us, grown in our Earth's soil, ferried from across the world, right to our homes and fresh for us to eat. Savour the aroma of herbs as you cook, the smells and tastes you create. This is so you can learn to appreciate the little things. By immersing yourself fully in these experiences, you'll discover hidden joys and find peace in the simplest of tasks, releasing worries about the future and letting go of past regrets. You can unlock a gateway to endless joy.

Never forget to celebrate the happiness that flows from appreciating the everyday wonders that surround you, so listen to your inner child and infuse your day with playfulness. Sing in the shower, dance while making breakfast, or have a silly moment with your loved ones. Allow yourself to laugh and enjoy the simple pleasures that each day brings. Let playfulness be your sidekick on the journey to find joy.

As you take your time to enjoy the world around you in its present moment, you will be setting yourself free by letting go of old attachments. Release the weight of the past and the worries about the future that we carry simply through habit. Seize the freedom of the present moment, where you can fully immerse yourself in the joy of being alive. Leave space for spontaneity, playfulness, and unbridled happiness.

Congratulations on discovering the joy of being present! Embrace the magic that resides in everyday moments – the taste of food, the act of getting dressed, the drive to work. By engaging with each moment mindfully, you unlock a world of happiness and fulfilment. Let go of worries, savour the sensations, and find gratitude in the simplest things. May your life be filled with an abundance of magical moments and may joy be your faithful sidekick every step of the way.

Chapter 6

Loving Yourself and Taking Care: The Power of Me-Time

It's time to give yourself some serious love and care. Do you sometimes forget about yourself and your own needs? By having no boundaries set in place, do you have no time for the hobbies you used to enjoy and now put off because everything else has become more important?

Do you also feel that sometimes you just don't fit in or as chilled and relaxed as everyone else? This is probably because you have agreed to something that deep down you didn't really want to do, or you are trying to keep up with the crowd around you. Has this happened more than once? Maybe this is because you have monitored what's going on around you more than you follow your own dreams, and as a result, you end up not being true to your own needs, instead feeling drained and deflated.

Well, let's explore the importance of setting boundaries and nurturing healthy relationships. We'll also discover the superpower of self-compassion, where you'll learn to be kind to yourself no matter what. It's all about making self-care a priority and feeling awesome in your own skin.

Start by recognising your needs and values. Practise saying no when something doesn't align with your priorities or drains your energy. This may sound super easy or super difficult to all different individual personalities, but we can all become 'yes men' for different reasons. Some can be scared of missing out so will go along with anything, some can yearn to please family and friends, and some generally don't think before they commit to plans as they try to do everything. As a result, all end goals are not thought through according to what you really want to do in your own free time. Don't get me wrong, there are plenty of arrangements in life we have to commit to, but we always need to find space for our own spare time and to think about how we want to spend it.

Take a few minutes now, let your mind wonder through all the tasks or plans you would like to be doing. These may be small things like clearing and organising the house and getting rid of old unwanted clothes, raiding through paperwork you constantly put off, maybe starting some exercise to feel fit, or even something bigger like planning your first-ever small business doing a craft you really enjoy. It's time to fill in your prepared hourly planner and start planning your schedule with some of *you* in there! Take out your diary or calendar. Whether it's on paper or an app on your phone, if you don't work from a diary it is time to do so now! Another unrecognised superpower is pre-planning your days with what's important to you, as it is super productive to write down tasks you want to complete. Think to yourself, if you don't do this now, when will you ever find time?!

Setting boundaries in our hectic modern lives is crucial for maintaining mental and emotional well-being. Here are some tips to help you establish and maintain healthy boundaries:

Know Your Priorities; Identify your top priorities and values. This will help you determine where to allocate your time and energy, making it easier to say "no" to things that don't align with your goals.

Learn to Say "No": Practise saying "no" without feeling guilty. Remember, every "yes" to something means a "no" to something else. Be polite but firm in declining tasks or commitments that overwhelm you. Also try not to follow your "no" with an excuse as you owe it to yourself to be honest when setting boundaries. You don't want to be carrying guilt around with you for every "no" you give. Communicate your boundaries with clarity and confidence.

Manage Technology Use: Limit your screen time and establish technology-free zones, especially during meals and before bedtime. Create boundaries when it comes to work-related emails and notifications to prevent burnout.

Set Clear Work Hours: If possible, define specific work hours and stick to them. Avoid letting work bleed into personal time and vice versa.

Communicate Your Boundaries: Let others know about your boundaries, whether it's colleagues, friends, or family. Effective communication is key to ensuring others respect your limits. Don't feel the need to over-explain yourself though, just something as simple as "I need some me-time" or "I'm just doing me". This way you won't need to worry about anyone taking it personally.

Delegate and Seek Help: Don't be afraid to delegate tasks or ask for help when needed. You don't have to do everything yourself, and teamwork can lighten your load. We are all a little guilty of trying to take on everything then complain we have too much to do!

Schedule "Me-Time": Prioritise self-care by scheduling regular "me-time" for relaxation, hobbies, or activities that bring you joy and recharge your energy.

Practise Mindfulness: Engage in mindfulness techniques, such as meditation or deep breathing as we have learnt in Chapter 2, to stay present and reduce stress when things become overwhelming.

Limit Overcommitting: Be mindful of taking on too many responsibilities. Evaluate the impact of each commitment on your overall well-being before agreeing to take them on.

Self-compassion: Treat yourself with kindness, understanding, and forgiveness. Practise positive self-talk, replacing self-criticism with self-encouragement. Embrace the fact that making mistakes is part of being human and an opportunity for growth. Treat yourself as you would a dear friend, offering comfort, support, and unconditional love.

Self-Care: Create a self-care routine that nourishes your mind, body, and soul. Set aside dedicated time for activities that bring you joy and relaxation. It could be indulging in a warm bubble bath, practising yoga or meditation, journaling, reading a book, or engaging in a hobby you love. Prioritise self-care as an essential part of your daily life, replenishing your energy and boosting your overall well-being. If it's first thing in the morning or last thing at night, always find time for you.

Avoid Comparison: Recognise that everyone's life is different, and what works for others may not be suitable for you. This is a super important one – nowadays through social media, we see only the good things our contacts are up to, but remember, most people don't show the bad or boring side and we will never know what goes on behind closed doors. Try not to compare yourself to others and focus on setting boundaries that cater to your unique needs and circumstances.

Reevaluate Regularly: Life changes, and so can your boundaries. Regularly reassess your commitments and adjust your boundaries as needed to accommodate new situations and challenges. Remember, setting boundaries is an ongoing process. It is an act of self-respect and self-care, allowing you to maintain healthy relationships and preserve your well-being. It's okay to make adjustments as you learn what works best for you. Welcome the power of saying "yes" to yourself and "no" to unnecessary stress, and you'll navigate the modern world with greater ease and balance.

Celebrate your individuality: Recognise and appreciate your strengths, talents, and quirks. Explore your passions and pursue activities that bring you fulfilment. Surround yourself with a supportive community that appreciates your authentic self. You don't need a superhero cape to be recognised as a one-of-a-kind masterpiece. The world is brighter with your unique light shining.

Remember, Mindful Magic: Incorporate mindfulness into your daily life to fully experience the present moment. Practise deep breathing exercises to ground yourself in the here and now. Engage your senses by noticing the sights, sounds, smells, tastes, and textures around you. Whether you're savouring a cup of tea, taking a walk, or enjoying a delicious meal, be fully present and relish the simple pleasures. Mindfulness allows you to slow down, appreciate life's beauty, and cultivate a sense of gratitude with time for yourself.

Congratulations, superhero! By setting boundaries and nurturing healthy relationships, you can create a supportive environment that values your well-being. Through the superpower of self-compassion, you become your own greatest ally and source of love. Make self-care a priority, engaging in activities that replenish your energy and bring you joy. Embrace your unique superpowers, celebrate your individuality, and radiate self-confidence. With mindfulness, you can fully enjoy each moment and find gratitude in the everyday wonders of life. Accept the superpower of loving yourself and let your light shine brightly in the world. You deserve all the love and happiness that comes your way.

Chapter 7

Building a Supportive Squad: Connecting with Others

In this chapter, we'll uncover the beauty and importance of building a supportive community. Friends, therapists, or online groups can be your superpowers. We'll explore how opening up, being vulnerable, and finding people who understand can help you feel less alone. Get ready to meet amazing people who will cheer you on and share your journey.

We have delved deep into the importance of finding enjoyment in our own time, but this does not mean you need to spend your life alone without interactions from others. It's actually super important to communicate with other fellow humans. Now is the time to take a minute to reflect on our current circle of friends, work colleagues, and family members, and appreciate what imprint they have on our lives.

Life changes throughout the years, but we sometimes find it hard to face changes in our friendships. Just because you may have been friends with someone since school does not mean that you have to be there for them at their every beck and call. On our life journeys, we all change directions at different times and that may mean you don't always have the same interests or time commitments as each other and that's ok. Some of us are lucky enough to still have that long-term friend or have met great short-term mates. Life can feel amazing around them, but along the way, we can pick up some friendships that bring only negativity, absorbing our time and energy that could be useful elsewhere. This also is relevant to our families and work surroundings. Before we examine this topic in more detail, take a moment to reflect on the people close to you and, using the skills we have learnt in the last chapter about setting boundaries and saying no, think about how you can assert yourself and your goals.

The Power of Connection: Picture having a team of super sidekicks right beside you, always ready to support and uplift you. But how do you find these incredible allies? Well, one way is through friendships. Look for people who share your interests, values, and sense of humour. Build relationships based on trust and mutual support.

Take a step back from everyone and take some time to see how these friendships and relationships unveil without you giving your all. This takes time as the people around you will be so accustomed to your agreeable ways that they will all react differently. Time will show you your true meaningful relationships and soon you'll have a squad of friends who will be there for you through thick and thin without the unnecessary dramas.

Surround yourself with people who bring out the best in you. Nurture relationships that are built on love, respect, and genuine support. Choose friendships and partnerships where your uniqueness is celebrated and cherished. Share laughter, adventures, and meaningful conversations with those who uplift your spirits and contribute positively to your life.

Where to find your super squad

Community Events and Workshops: Attend local events, workshops, or seminars related to your interests or the areas you want to explore. These gatherings provide opportunities to meet like-minded individuals who may become lifelong friends or valuable members of your support squad. Take part in group activities, strike up conversations, and be open to forming new connections.

Therapist Extraordinaire: Sometimes, we need a little extra help from a professional. This could sound like nonsense to you, or it may be something you have already sought in your life.

How we have been brought up or the people with whom we surround ourselves shapes our current opinion of talking to a professional about our problems, thoughts, and feelings, but believe me, they are *professional.* They do their jobs because they want to help people, creating a safe space where you can talk without being judged, knowing that they will never repeat any of your conversations. You don't need to tell anyone that you are speaking to a counsellor or therapist, and you will be surprised how good you will feel after just one session.

Finding a therapist who understands your needs and can provide guidance is like discovering a secret superpower. Start by researching therapists in your area or seek recommendations from trusted sources. Don't be afraid to reach out and schedule a first consultation, as these are normally free. Remember, choosing the right therapist is about finding someone you feel comfortable opening up to and who can support you on your journey to mental well-being. There are a huge number of specialists offering a varied choice of support that you may find helpful. You might find charities in your local area that offer free advice. This can be a good place to discover what support you need. You may find some counsellors or therapists are more spiritual or religious than others, which can sometimes help in finding the right one for you.

It can be helpful to seek recommendations from friends, family, or healthcare professionals. They may know of someone who specialises in the areas in which you're seeking support.

Personal recommendations can give you a sense of trust and confidence in your choice. Utilise online directories or platforms that connect you with therapists specialising in your specific needs. Many websites provide comprehensive profiles and client reviews, helping you make an informed decision. Take your time to research and compare therapists before reaching out for an initial consultation.

Online Allies: In today's digital age, online communities and support groups can be a powerful source of connection and understanding. Join forums or social media groups that align with your interests or specific challenges. Engage in conversations, ask questions, and share your experiences. These virtual spaces can be a lifeline, offering advice, encouragement, and a sense of belonging from people who truly get you. You may find that watching online videos about positive thinking, letting go of the past, or discovering a "new you" will help you open up to a world of change and give you some great inspiration.

Your super sidekicks are out there! If you need allies right now, here are some of my favourite recommendations of where to look:

1. **Supportive Friends:** Build a strong network of friends by being open, genuine, and present in your relationships. Foster an environment of trust and non-judgment, where everyone feels comfortable sharing their thoughts and emotions. Actively listen and offer support when your friends reach out. Remember, being a friend means being there through the ups and downs, offering a shoulder to lean on and a cheering squad for their dreams.

2. **Local Support Groups:** Check out local community or counselling centres or churches for support groups addressing topics you're interested in. These groups bring together individuals facing similar challenges, allowing you to connect, share experiences, and gain support from people who understand firsthand what you're going through. The power of shared experiences can be transformative.

3. **Online Communities:** Explore online platforms and social media groups dedicated to mental health, personal growth,

or specific interests. Participate in discussions, share your own experiences, and lend a supportive ear to others. These virtual communities provide a space to connect with individuals from all walks of life, offering encouragement, advice, and a sense of belonging.

Your Super Squad Awaits

Congratulations, superhero! Building a supportive squad is within your grasp. Seek out friends who align with your values and interests, forming a network of trust and support. When it comes to finding a therapist, rely on recommendations, online resources, and community events to discover the right fit for your needs. Explore online communities, where you can connect with like-minded individuals who provide empathy and understanding. Remember, supporting others is just as important as receiving support. Be there for your friends, offer encouragement, and celebrate their successes. Engage in local support groups and online communities where you can find people who truly understand your journey. Your super squad are a massive power boost and are there to share experiences and remind you that you're never alone. Together, you can navigate life's challenges, celebrate joys, and create a supportive network that uplifts and empowers each member. Embrace the power of connection, and let your squad be the best superpowers in your life.

Chapter 8

Unleashing the Power of Attraction: Manifesting Your Dreams

Welcome to the grand finale of our soulful adventure! Get ready to dive into the captivating world of the Law of Attraction, where your thoughts become the power that manifests your wildest dreams.

In this epic finale, you'll discover that you are the ultimate creator of your own reality. So, put on your manifestation cape, sprinkle a dash of faith and belief, and get ready to manifest your dreams. The universe is eagerly waiting to bring your desires to life – let's make some magic happen!

The Law of Attraction

Here's how it works: You're a superhero and your thoughts are your superpower. When you think positive thoughts, you send good vibes into the universe. And guess what? The universe loves good vibes! It starts conspiring to give you all the fantastic things you desire.

But wait, there's more! The Law of Attraction isn't just about thinking positively. It's about feeling positive too. When you feel happy, excited, and grateful, your vibes become even stronger, like a superhero in full force.

So, imagine you want to find a new job. Instead of worrying or doubting, you focus on what you want – a fulfilling job that makes your heart sing. You visualise yourself in that dream job, feeling the excitement of success. You radiate gratitude for the job you know is coming your way.

And here's the super cool part: As you maintain your positive thoughts and feelings, the universe starts to align for you. You might receive unexpected job offers, meet the right people who can help, or stumble upon the perfect opportunity. It's like the universe is saying, "Here you go, hero! Your dream job awaits!"

But remember, just like any superhero, you also need to take action. You can't sit back and wait for everything to fall into your lap. You gotta put on your cape, step out into the world, and make things happen. The Law of Attraction loves someone who acts!

So, embrace your superpower, think positive thoughts, feel the joy, and take inspired action. Trust that the universe has your back, and watch as your dreams become a reality. You're the creator of your own adventure, my friend, so go out there and make it extraordinary!

Here's the simple science behind it:

1. **Thoughts:** Your thoughts are like signals that you send out into the universe. They carry a specific frequency or vibration. When you consistently focus on positive thoughts, you emit positive vibrations.

2. **Emotions:** Emotions are like the fuel behind your thoughts. They give your thoughts a stronger charge and intensity. When you feel positive emotions like joy, gratitude, and excitement, you amplify the power of your thoughts and vibrations.

3. **Energy:** Everything in the universe is made up of energy, including your thoughts and emotions. This energy radiates outward and interacts with the energy of the universe. Like attracts like – positive energy attracts positive experiences.

4. **Quantum Physics:** Quantum physics suggests that everything is connected at a fundamental level. The energy you release through your thoughts and emotions interacts with the energy of the universe, creating a magnetic attraction. It's like a cosmic dance whenever similar vibrations come together.

5. **Resonance**: When your thoughts and emotions align with the frequency of what you desire, you create a resonance – a harmonious match. This resonance attracts experiences, opportunities, and people that align with your desires.

6. **Action:** The Law of Attraction isn't just about wishful thinking; it's about taking inspired action. When you align

your thoughts, emotions, and energy, you become more open and receptive to the opportunities and synchronicities that come your way. You become an active participant in manifesting your desires.

So, in simple terms, the Law of Attraction works by aligning your thoughts, emotions, and energy with whatever you want to attract. It's like tuning your radio to a specific frequency to hear the songs you love. When you think positively, feel good, and take inspired action, you create a magnetic field that draws in the experiences and opportunities that match your desires. You become the co-creator of your reality, shaping your life in a way that brings you joy, abundance, and fulfilment.

Understanding the logic and science behind the law of attraction reveals that our thousands of daily thoughts offer us our life's reality. Remember, you hold the power to attract all that your heart desires. The journey doesn't end here; it's just the beginning of a life filled with abundance, joy, and infinite possibilities. Get ready to soar into a world where your dreams become your reality!

Positive affirmations are like that strike of lightning or that radioactive spider bite that can transform us from everyday people and unleash the inner superhero within us. These uplifting mantras remind us that we are worthy, capable, and oh-so-amazing, even on days when we feel more like sleepy sloths! By repeating these affirmations, we send the signal to our subconscious that we believe in ourselves, boosting confidence and banishing self-doubt to the land of the forgotten. Positive affirmations are the secret recipe for a potion that can summon courage and cultivate self-love. So, sprinkle those affirmations like confetti and watch as they weave their power, turning every challenge into an opportunity for greatness!

Here are some positive affirmations for you to try. Choose at least 5 that resonate with you the most and repeat them to yourself either out loud or in your head. Even better, stand in front of the mirror and look at yourself whilst repeating these affirmations so you watch your smile grow and your heart fill with self-love. Go on, give it a try. Do this daily, adding a new positive affirmation to your list each day.

I am worthy of love and happiness.

I believe in my abilities and embrace all challenges.

I am confident and capable of achieving my goals.

Every day, I grow stronger and more resilient.

I am surrounded by positive energy and supportive people.

I am in control of my thoughts and emotions.

I radiate positivity and attract good things into my life.

I am deserving of success and abundance.

I am grateful for all the blessings in my life.

I am a magnet for opportunities and prosperity.

I am beautiful inside and out.

I am constantly evolving and becoming a better version of myself.

I am at peace with my past and excited for my future.

I am filled with confidence and grace in all situations.

I am open to receiving love and kindness from others.

I am courageous and can face any challenge that comes my way.

I trust in the universe's plan for me.

I am worthy of achieving my dreams and aspirations.

I am a source of positivity and inspiration to those around me.

I am grateful for the gift of life and embrace each moment with joy.

The Adventure Within: Embracing Your Soul's Journey

Congratulations! You've reached the end of your superhero journey! We've learnt how to nurture our minds, find peace in the chaos, and connect with ourselves and others. Remember, taking care of your mental health is a lifelong endeavour. So, keep exploring, trying new things, and embracing the adventure within. You've got this!

I hope you have enjoyed reading this self-help guide and now realise that change is possible. You are not alone in the world with your thoughts, feelings, and emotions as we all have them! With just one step at a time, you can calm your mind and nurture your soul, creating more happiness for yourself. You will be rewarded with the best superhero version of you there is.

Printed in Great Britain
by Amazon